DATE DUE			
AUG 5 '92	JAN 8 03		
FEB 15 '94			
APR 11 94			
MAY 29 '95			
JAN 28 97			
OCT 0 6 99			
FEB 4 00			
AUG 2 8 00			
JAN 31 '00			
APR 29 00			
JUN 14 02			

A NIGHT AND DAY IN THE DESERT

Jennifer Owings Dewey

Little, Brown and Company
Boston Toronto London

This book is dedicated to my friend Rosalind Constable

Other books by Jennifer Owings Dewey

Birds of Antarctica: The Adélie Penguin
Birds of Antarctica: The Wandering Albatross
At the Edge of the Pond

First edition

Library of Congress Cataloging-in-Publication Data

Dewey, Jennifer.
   A night and day in the desert / Jennifer Owings Dewey.—1st ed.
     p.   cm.
   Summary: Depicts the unique environment of the desert, with its
plant and animal life and special climatic conditions.
   ISBN 0-316-18210-9
   1. Desert biology—Juvenile literature. 2. Deserts—Juvenile
literature. [1. Desert biology. 2. Deserts.] I. Title.
QH88.D48   1991
574.909′54—dc20   89-13697
                                          CIP
                                           AC

10 9 8 7 6 5 4 3 2 1

WOR

Published simultaneously in Canada
by Little, Brown & Company (Canada) Limited

Printed in the United States of America

When sundown comes to the desert, the silence of early evening is broken by a series of short barks and ringing cries, followed by yipping and yapping. A long, shrill chorus rolls over the desert, one coyote singing to another.

Pointing her nose to the sky, a female coyote calls her mate, half a mile away. He answers with a howl of his own. Night is coming, and it is time to hunt.

The coyote pair join together, walking soundlessly in soft sand on a path circling a lava plateau. The lava, a pile of black volcanic rock forty feet high and a mile wide, is 250,000 years old. Windblown sand and soil, accumulated over centuries, form shallow banks and shoals where plants take root. Grasses and plants provide cover for animals hunting on the lava.

Leaving the path, the coyote pair climb the lava, stepping on rocks still warm from the sun. Their sleek coats shimmer in the fading light as they thread their way through stands of yucca and thorny ocotillo, avoiding patches of prickly pear and barrel cactus.

In the desert an animal's survival often depends on how visible it is. Lava rock is black. On black rock, animals have adapted their colors so they blend with their environment. Roadrunners living on lava have dark feathers, rattlesnakes have dark scales.

Coyotes prey on rodents but will eat anything, including frogs and snakes. Wood rats, kangaroo rats, horned lizards, and jackrabbits, all good food to a coyote, find sanctuary under tangled plant growth on the lava. Millipedes, trap-door spiders, and darkling beetles burrow under spiny brush, safely hidden.

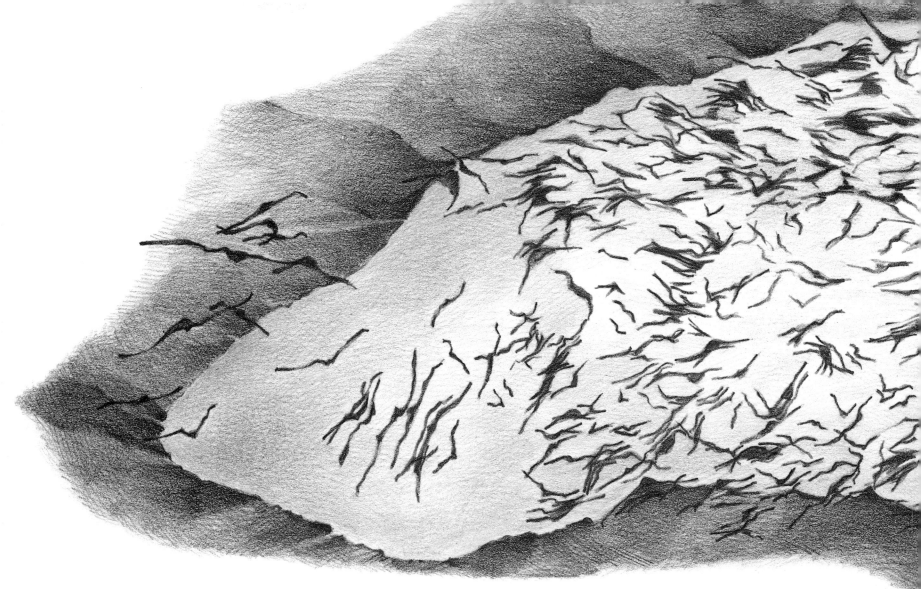

As night falls, a half-moon appears behind distant sand hills. In a cave in the lava plateau one million Mexican free-tailed bats hang upside down, suspended from the cave ceiling by long claws on their hind legs. The bats are restless, stirred by a signal known only to them. Rustling bat wings fill the gloomy chamber with soft murmurings. Whistles, squeaks, and flutterings rebound off cave walls as bats let go, drop from the roof, and swarm out a fifteen-foot-wide cave entrance. Bats fly from stagnant, murky darkness into a luminous twilight sky. Only mothers with newborns, and babies too young to fly, stay behind.

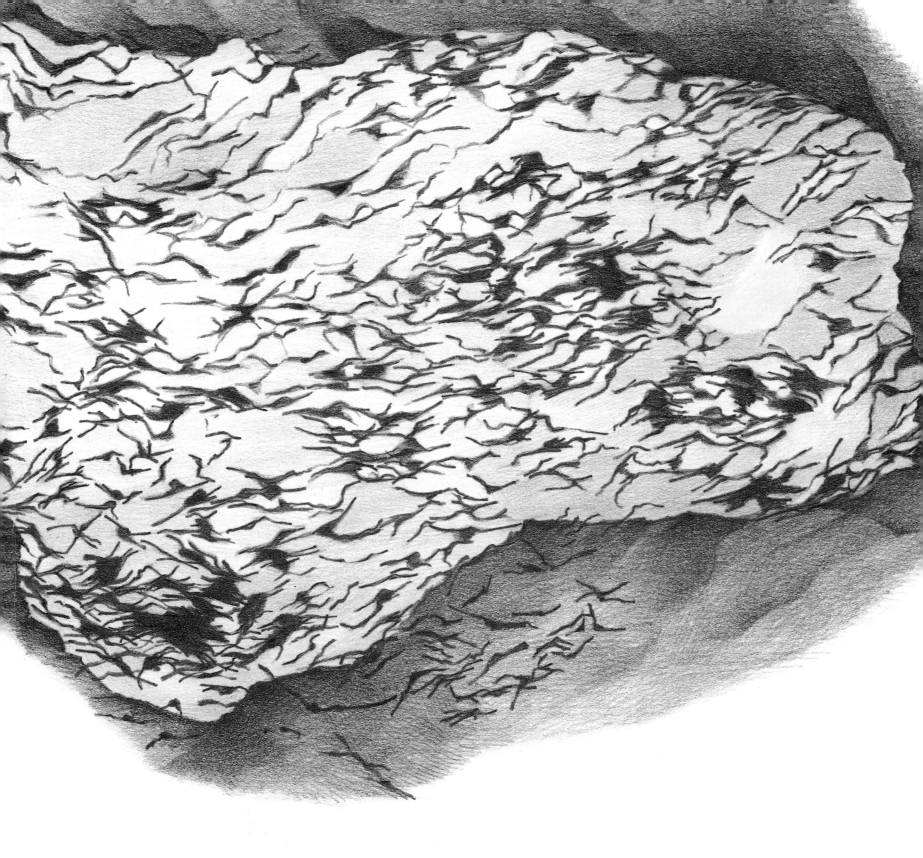

There are so many bats that it takes one hour for all of them to fly through the narrow cave opening. Yet even with thousands ascending into the air at once, freetails rarely bump each other in flight. Elusive and quick, bats have an uncanny sense of where they are, and where home is. Bats are mammals, and they see quite well with their eyes, but they bounce sound off objects around them and listen for echoes. They use this echolocation to find their way, and to find insect prey.

Freetails have a ten-inch wingspan but weigh only half an ounce. Delicate skin membranes, stretching between body, arms, and legs, form their wings. A tail extending past the back membrane gives freetails their name. The tail membrane is used to spoon insects out of the air in mid-flight. In one gesture, freetails lift the tail membrane to their mouth to eat a captured insect.

In the clear desert air the bat flight is visible for two miles. Lofty predators see the bats and gather over the cave. Great horned owls and Swainson's hawks, gliding on silent wings, seize bats with sharp talons and eat on the wing.

Rising ten thousand feet into the sky, the bat column leaves the hungry raptors behind. Sixty-mile-an-hour winds help bats cover one hundred miles of desert in search of food. Freetails live on a diet of insects. By dawn the bats will return to roosts in the cave, having eaten a ton of insects.

At night, when the desert cools off, animals leave their dens, nests, and shelters to go in search of food, water, and mates.

Near the bat cave opening a spring drips water into a natural bowl in the lava. Condensed moisture, drawn from underground on air currents, rises through tunnels in the lava. It trickles and pools at the surface, creating a miniature water hole. Beds of emerald moss, no bigger than thumbnails, edge the water. The pool is an oasis on parched, sunbaked rock, and animals come to use it.

Most animals, like antelope and skunk, must drink or they will die. Yet some desert animals, like kangaroo rats, never need to drink. Moisture in seeds they eat is metabolized completely by bodies able to conserve water.

By the edge of the pool the measured throb and cadence of insect wings blend with the shuffle and thump of rabbit feet.

Dark scales quivering, flat head sliding, a western diamondback rattlesnake, three feet long, dips a forked tongue in the pool. Wary and shy, a fox stops to drink. Bats dart over the pool. Ripples on the water show they have taken a drink.

Nearing the pool, the coyote pair surprise wolf spiders and centipedes, sending the insects scurrying for cover. Both animals lower their head, at water's edge, and sip. Refreshed, they turn and move away, one behind the other, striding down a rocky slope, bodies lean, powerful, and tireless. In a single night they may walk fifteen miles in search of food.

Mice are plentiful on earth, especially in the desert. Seeds of desert plants wait years for enough rain to germinate. Falling on the ground, seeds of wild grasses, rabbitbrush, and yucca provide abundant food for small rodents.

Pocket mice, pocket gophers, and kangaroo rats use fur-lined cheek pouches for carrying seeds to caches underground. Desert rodents disperse seeds by stashing, storing, and spreading them. Mice harvest seeds in summer. Their caches are insurance against lean times.

Weaving noiselessly among lava boulders is a ring-tailed cat, its huge eyes glowing in the dark.

Under a pile of prickly pear, a spiny pocket mouse senses the ringtail is near. Shivering nervously, the mouse involuntarily squeaks. Alerted by the sound, sniffing warm, strong mouse smell, the ringtail pounces. Escape is impossible. The mouse is caught in needle-sharp teeth, its skull pierced.

The ringtail turns, disappearing into shadows in the rocks, the mouse clenched in its teeth.

A male red-kneed tarantula, legs spreading six inches, crawls from a silk-lined burrow in the sand. Searching for food and a mate, the tarantula is solitary, a lone hunter. His venom, harmless to humans, is instantly fatal to small rodents, lizards, and insects.

By the water hole on the lava, the male tarantula meets a red-kneed female. He lifts two hairy front legs in the air as his eight eyes glint. Distracting the female with his movements, the male mates with her, pulling away quickly afterward. If given the chance, the female will kill and eat him.

A banner-tailed kangaroo rat, silky-furred, beady-eyed, tail flying, shoots over the sand and up the lava plateau. Briefly, male tarantula and rat face each other. The spider throws up his front legs, this time in defense. The rat races on.

Near the bat cave entrance the rat meets a black-tailed rattlesnake.

Startled, off guard, the snake loses a crucial second before pivoting a deadly head in the air to strike.

The rat is quick, leaping twenty feet past the snake's head in a bound. Landing, the rat leaps a second time, and a third. Out of reach, the rat is safe.

With a soft thud the snake's head touches the rocks. Turning its body length, scales trembling, the snake glides effortlessly into inky shadows in the bat cave.

A pungent odor hangs in the cave, sweet-sour bat smell mixed with fumes rising off layers of guano, or bat droppings, on the cave floor. Dermestid beetles crawl on the guano, feeding on the flesh of fallen bats. Less than a quarter-inch long, scaly and dull-colored, dermestids lay eggs on guano. The beetle larvae, like parent beetles, feed on bats that have toppled from above and cannot launch themselves into flight again.

Skillful flyers, freetails have weak arm and leg bones, not made for walking. It is nearly impossible for them to take off from the ground or regain the cave roof once they have fallen.

Near dawn, as the bats enter the cave, one after another, they drop like stones from the sky. Darting in through the opening, they find a place and hook on. Pink, hairless baby bats clinging to the darkest part of the ceiling wait for mother bats to return and nurse them. Mother bats identify their offspring by their baby's unique, high-pitched cry.

Once attached to the ceiling, bats settle in for a day of sleep, digesting the night's take of insects, three hundred bats to a square foot of cave ceiling.

The coyote pair return to their dens as morning light streaks the sky red, then yellow. Both animals are still hungry, the night's hunting only partly successful. In the heat of the day they will sleep, waiting for sundown to hunt again.

Five gray-brown coyote pups crowd the opening of the female's den, wiggling and squirming and whimpering in anticipation of her arrival. Latching their mouths to her nipples, the pups nurse while she dozes off. Four weeks earlier, when the pups were born, their father moved out, into a den of his own. He continues to hunt with his mate and brings food to the pups when he can.

The word "desert" comes from the Latin word for "abandoned." As dawn becomes late morning, and then midday, the desert looks abandoned. Intense heat drives desert dwellers into dens, burrows, and hiding places. Sunlight shines on wind-rippled sand, dry lake beds, salt flats, and gullies where water seldom runs. The land is stark, a hot, dry place where less than ten inches of rain falls in a year.

At midday few creatures stir. Grasshoppers and cicadas confer with raspy wing rubbings. An eight-inch desert tortoise lumbers over the sand, stopping to chew creosote leaves, leaving distinctive tracks behind. Pronghorn antelope, in groups of three or four, graze sparse grasses. Jackrabbits hop from sagebrush to sagebrush, always on the shady side. A cactus wren adds fresh grass to her already bulky nest.

On the path by the lava plateau a two-foot-long roadrunner chases a prairie rattlesnake, a favorite prey of roadrunners. The snake is no match for the roadrunner. Nimble and fast, the roadrunner captures the snake seconds before it can plunge down a gopher hole. Roadrunners outwit, and outlast, rattlesnakes, earning the nickname snakebird.

Afternoon heat shimmers, glints, and blazes on sand and rock. As the day's heat builds, even jackrabbits find places to lie down and rest. Hot air rises to great altitudes, meeting cold air. Storms build up, storms carried on strong winds. By late afternoon, dark, heavy clouds obscure a lowering sun. Fingers of lightning flash, thunder booms. Winds blow a thunderstorm over the desert.

Rain on the desert is rare. Animals with short lives, like rodents, lizards, and insects, sometimes never know rain, since their lives begin and end before rain comes.

Suddenly the ground is awash in a cloudburst of sudden violence. Rain runs in torrents down arroyos. Mud and uprooted plants flow in gullies. Water pours in ruddy streams off rocks. Animals are swept from burrows, insects flooded from holes.

Waves of rain sweep over dunes and buttes, touching down, moving on, all in twenty minutes.

The desert responds exuberantly to rain. Seeds burst open, roots and tendrils soak up water, cactus flesh swells, every cell made to store water. Dry soil turns to slick and slippery mud. After a good rain the desert blooms and buzzes, and the spadefoot toad appears.

Spiny projections on hind feet give the spadefoot its name. In dry times the toad digs backward in the soil, surrounding itself with a jellylike substance made by its own body. The toad lies dormant for as long as eight or nine months. Awakened by a cloudburst, the toad comes to, digs out, and heads for the nearest puddle. After rain is the only time the spadefoot appears. Timing is crucial. Mating and egg laying must take place before the puddle dries up.

Sitting mid-puddle, croaking loudly, male spadefoot toads attract females. In minutes eggs are fertilized, in two days eggs hatch.

In a week to ten days toadlets find their way to mud at the bottom of the drying puddle, able to dig their own retreats.

A flame of light from the setting sun lingers in a sky blown clean of clouds. The dazzling glare of day is gone. Darkness falls, the moon rises. The coyotes leave their dens, stand on brushy ridges, and call each other, their yipping and yapping signaling the start of a night of hunting. Bats again fly from the cave, whirling like smoke in the sky.

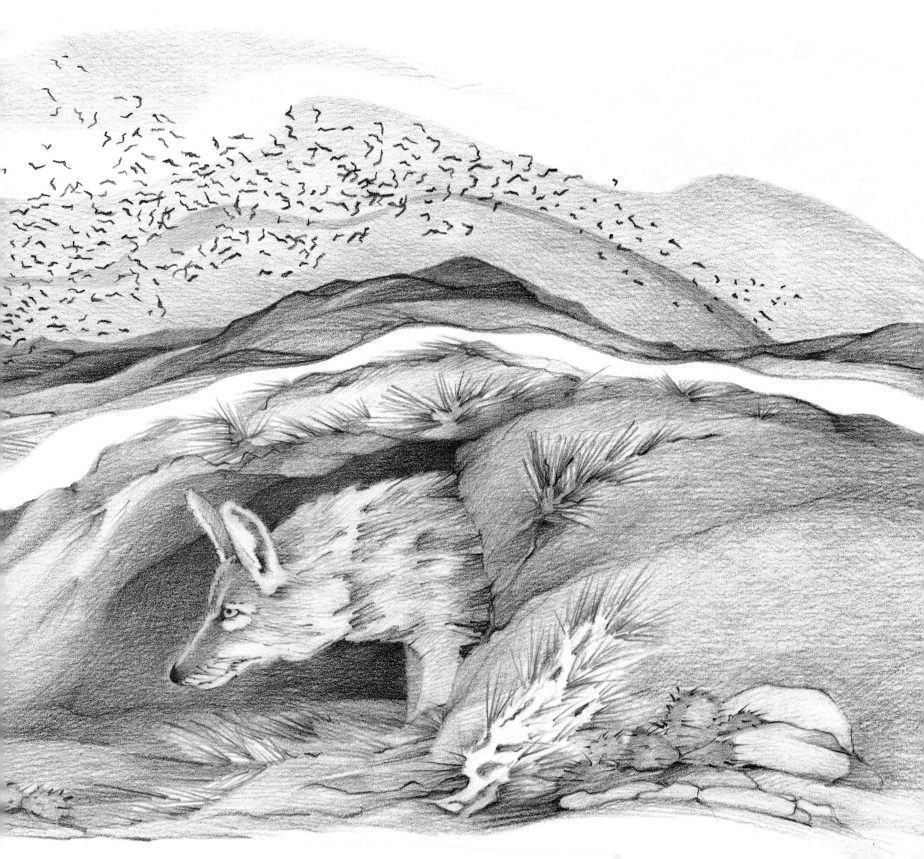

Aroused by an urge to fill an empty stomach, find water or a mate, desert animals and insects emerge from nests, dens, burrows, holes, and hiding places. Another desert night begins.